MW00748749

Celebrity
BABY *fashion*

Celebrity babies are big news, and all eyes are on what they're wearing. These crochet fashions let you "get the look" seen when the stars have ventured out on family days.

2   6   10

13   18   23

26   31   35

LEISURE ARTS, INC. • Maumelle, Arkansas

COWL

EASY

SHOPPING LIST

Yarn (Medium Weight)

[3.5 ounces, 170 yards
(100 grams, 156 meters) per
skein]:

- ☐ Dk Pink - 1 skein
- ☐ White - 1 skein

Crochet Hook

- ☐ Size I (5.5 mm)

  or size needed for gauge

SIZE INFORMATION

Finished Neck Circumference:

Small (3-12 mos): 17¼" (44 cm)

Large (12-24 mos): 20" (51 cm)

Finished Length:

Small (3-12 mos): 8½" (21.5 cm)

Large (12-24 mos): 9½" (24 cm)

Size Note: We have printed
the instructions for the sizes in
different colors to make it easier
for you to find:

Small in Blue

Large in Green

Instructions in Black apply to both
sizes.

GAUGE INFORMATION

In pattern, two repeats
   (18 sts) = 5¾" (14.5 cm);
   6 rnds = 4" (10 cm)
   9 sc and 12 rows = 3" (7.5 cm)

Gauge Swatch: 3" (7.5 cm) square
With White, ch 10.

Row 1: Sc in second ch from hook
and in each ch across: 9 sc.

Rows 2-12: Ch 1, turn; sc in each sc
across.

Finish off.

— STITCH GUIDE —

 **DOUBLE CROCHET
2 TOGETHER**
(abbreviated dc2tog)
(uses next 2 sts)

★ YO, insert hook in **next** st, YO
and pull up a loop, YO and draw
through 2 loops on hook; repeat
from ★ once **more**, YO and draw
through all 3 loops on hook
(counts as one dc).

INSTRUCTIONS
Body

With White, ch 54{63} **loosely**; being careful **not** to twist ch, join with slip st to form a ring.

Rnd 1 (Right side)**:** Ch 1, sc in same ch as joining and in each ch around; join with slip st to first sc: 54{63} sc.

Note: Loop a short piece of yarn around any stitch to mark Rnd 1 as **right** side.

Rnd 2: Ch 1, sc in same st as joining and in each sc around; join with slip st to first sc, finish off.

Rnd 3: With **right** side facing, ▀▄ join Dk Pink with dc in any sc *(see Joining With Dc, page 40)*; 2 dc in same st, dc2tog 4 times, (5 dc in next sc, dc2tog 4 times) around, 2 dc in same st as first dc; join with slip st to first dc.

Rnd 4: Ch 3 (**counts as first dc**), 2 dc in same st as joining, dc2tog 4 times, (5 dc in next dc, dc2tog 4 times) around, 2 dc in same st as first dc; join with slip st to first dc.

Repeat Rnd 4 for pattern until Body measures approximately 7¼{8¼}"/18.5{21} cm from beginning ch.

Finish off.

Edging

Rnd 1: With **right** side facing,  join White with sc in same st as joining *(see Joining With Sc, page 40)*; sc in each dc around; join with slip st to first sc, finish off: 54{63} sc.

Rnd 2: With **right** side facing, join Dk Pink with dc in same st as joining; 2 dc in same st, dc2tog 4 times, (5 dc in next sc, dc2tog 4 times) around, 2 dc in same st as first dc; join with slip st to first dc, finish off.

Rnd 3: With **right** side facing, join White with sc in same st as joining; sc in each dc around; join with slip st to first sc.

Rnd 4: Ch 1, sc in same st as joining and in each sc around; join with slip st to first sc, finish off.

NEWSBOY HAT

 **EASY**

SIZE INFORMATION

Finished Head Circumference:

Small (3-12 mos): 13½" (34.5 cm)

Medium (12-18 mos): 15¼"
(38.5 cm)

Large (18-24 mos): 16¾" (42.5 cm)

Size Note: We have printed
the instructions for the sizes in
different colors to make it easier
for you to find:

• Small in Blue

• Medium in Pink

• Large in Green

Instructions in Black apply to all
sizes.

GAUGE INFORMATION

With larger size hook, in pattern,
15 sts and 8 rnds = 4" (10 cm)

Gauge Swatch:
3¼" (8.25 cm) diameter
Work same as Body through Rnd 3:
35 dc.

——— STITCH GUIDE ———

 **SINGLE CROCHET
2 TOGETHER**
(abbreviated sc2tog)
(uses next 2 sts)

Pull up a loop in each of next 2 sts,
YO and draw through all 3 loops
on hook (**counts as one sc**).

INSTRUCTIONS
Body

With larger size hook, ch 5; join
with slip st to form a ring.

Rnd 1 (Right side)**:** Ch 4 (**counts
as first dc plus ch 1**), (dc in ring,
ch 1) 6 times; join with slip st to
first dc: 7 dc and 7 ch-1 sps.

Note: Loop a short piece of yarn around any stitch to mark Rnd 1 as **right** side.

Rnd 2: Ch 3 **(counts as first dc, now and throughout)**, 2 dc in same st as joining, ch 1, (3 dc in next dc, ch 1) around; join with slip st to first dc: 21 dc and 7 ch-1 sps.

Rnd 3: Ch 3, 2 dc in same st as joining, skip next dc, 2 dc in next dc, ★ 3 dc in next dc, skip next dc, 2 dc in next dc; repeat from ★ around; join with slip st to first dc: 35 dc.

Rnd 4: Slip st in next 2 dc, ch 3, 2 dc in same st, skip next dc, 4 dc in next dc, ★ skip next 2 dc, 3 dc in next dc, skip next dc, 4 dc in next dc; repeat from ★ around; join with slip st to first dc: 49 dc.

Size Small ONLY

Rnd 5: Ch 3, 2 dc in same st as joining, skip next dc, 3 dc in next dc, (skip next 2 dc, 3 dc in next dc) 7 times, skip next dc, (3 dc in next dc, skip next 2 dc) around; join with slip st to first dc: 51 dc.

Size Medium ONLY

Rnd 5: Slip st in next 2 dc, ch 3, 2 dc in same st, (skip next dc, 3 dc in next dc) twice, skip next 2 dc, 3 dc in next dc, ★ skip next dc, 3 dc in next dc, (skip next 2 dc, 3 dc in next dc) twice, skip next dc, 3 dc in next dc, skip next 2 dc, 3 dc in next dc; repeat from ★ 2 times **more**; join with slip st to first dc: 57 dc.

Size Large ONLY

Rnd 5: Slip st in next 2 dc, ch 3, 2 dc in same st, skip next 2 dc, 3 dc in each of next 2 dc, ★ skip next 2 dc, 3 dc in next dc, skip next 2 dc, 3 dc in each of next 2 dc; repeat from ★ around; join with slip st to first dc: 63 dc.

All Sizes

Rnds 6 thru 9{10-11}: Slip st in next 2 dc, ch 3, 2 dc in same st, (skip next 2 dc, 3 dc in next dc) around; join with slip st to first dc, do **not** finish off.

Brim

Change to smaller size hook.

Row 1: Ch 1, beginning in same st as joining, sc2tog, sc in next 4 dc, 2 sc in next dc, ★ sc in next 7{8-9} dc, 2 sc in next dc; repeat from ★ once **more**, sc in next 4 dc, sc2tog, leave remaining 22{26-30} dc unworked: 30{32-34} sc.

Row 2: Ch 1, turn; beginning in first sc, sc2tog, sc in each sc across to last 2 sc, sc2tog: 28{30-32} sc.

Row 3: Ch 1, turn; beginning in first sc, sc2tog, sc in next 5 sc, 2 sc in next sc, sc in next 12{14-16} sc, 2 sc in next sc, sc in next 5 sc, sc2tog.

Row 4: Ch 1, turn; beginning in first sc, sc2tog, sc in each sc across to last 2 sc, sc2tog: 26{28-30} sc.

Row 5: Ch 1, turn; beginning in first sc, sc2tog, sc in next 5 sc, 2 sc in next sc, sc in next 10{12-14} sc, 2 sc in next sc, sc in next 5 sc, sc2tog.

Row 6: Ch 1, turn; beginning in first sc, sc2tog, sc in each sc across to last 2 sc, sc2tog: 24{26-28} sc.

Row 7: Ch 1, turn; beginning in first sc, sc2tog twice, sc in each sc across to last 4 sc, sc2tog twice: 20{22-24} sc.

Edging Rnd: Ch 1, do **not** turn; sc evenly across end of rows on Brim; sc in each unworked dc across last rnd of Body; sc evenly across end of rows on Brim; working in sts on Row 7 of Brim, 2 sc in first sc, sc in each sc across to last sc, 2 sc in last sc; join with slip st to first sc, finish off.

PONCHO

 **EASY**

SHOPPING LIST

Yarn

(Super Bulky Weight)
[3.5 ounces, 86 yards
(100 grams, 78 meters) per
skein]:

☐ Pink - 1 skein

☐ Variegated - 1 skein

Crochet Hook

☐ Size L (8 mm)

or size needed for gauge

Additional Supplies

☐ Yarn needle

GAUGE INFORMATION

In pattern,

(2 dc, ch 1) twice = 3" (7.5 cm);

8 dc and 4 rows/rnds = 4" (10 cm)

(sc, ch 1) 3 times =2½" (6.25 cm)

Gauge Swatch: 4" (10 cm) square

With Pink, ch 10.

Row 1: Dc in fourth ch from hook
(3 skipped chs count as first dc)
and in each ch across: 8 dc.

Rows 2-4: Ch 3 **(counts as first dc)**,
turn; dc in next dc and in each dc
across.

Finish off.

SIZE INFORMATION

Finished Neck Circumference:

Small (3-12 mos): 15" (38 cm)

Large (12-24 mos): 17½" (44.5 cm)

Size Note: We have printed
the instructions for the sizes in
different colors to make it easier
for you to find:

• Small in Blue

• Large in Green

Instructions in Black apply to both
sizes.

INSTRUCTIONS
Body

With Pink and beginning at neck
edge, ch 36{41}; being careful **not**
to twist ch, join with slip st to form
a ring.

Rnd 1 (Right side): Ch 1, sc in same
ch as joining and in each ch around;
join with slip st to first sc: 36{41} sc.

Note: Loop a short piece of yarn
around any stitch to mark Rnd 1 as
right side.

11

Rnd 2: Ch 3 **(counts as first dc, now and throughout)**, dc in next 7 sc, 2 dc in next sc, ★ dc in next 8{7} sc, 2 dc in next sc; repeat from ★ around; join with slip st to first dc: 40{46} dc.

Rnd 3: Ch 3, dc in same st as joining, ch 1, skip next dc, ★ 2 dc in next dc, ch 1, skip next dc; repeat from ★ around; join with slip st to first dc: 40{46} dc and 20{23} ch-1 sps.

Rnds 4 thru 6{7}: Slip st in next dc and in next ch-1 sp, ch 3, dc in same sp, ch 1, (2 dc in next ch-1 sp, ch 1) around; join with slip st to first dc.

Finish off.

Bottom Edging

With **right** side of last rnd facing, join Variegated with sc in any ch-1 sp *(see Joining With Sc, page 40)*; dc in next dc, 2 dc in next dc, ★ sc in next ch-1 sp, dc in next dc, 2 dc in next dc; repeat from ★ around; join with slip st to first sc, finish off.

Neck Edging

With **right** side facing and working in free loops of beginning ch *(Fig. 2b, page 40)*, join Variegated with sc in any ch; ch 1, ★ skip next ch, sc in next ch, ch 1; repeat from ★ around to last 1{0} ch(s) *(see Zeros, page 39)*, skip last 1{0} ch(s); join with slip st to first sc, finish off.

Flower

With Variegated and leaving a long end for sewing, ch 5; join with slip st to form a ring.

Rnd 1 (Right side)**:** Ch 1, (sc, ch 1, dc, ch 1) 5 times in ring; join with slip st to first sc, finish off.

Note: Mark Rnd 1 as **right** side.

Using photo as a guide for placement, sew **wrong** side of Flower to **right** side of Poncho.

HOODED SCARF

EASY +

SHOPPING LIST

Yarn (Medium Weight)

[5 ounces, 256 yards
(141 grams, 234 meters) per
skein]:
- ☐ Lavender - 1 skein

[4 ounces, 204 yards
(113 grams, 187 meters) per
skein]:
- ☐ Variegated - 1 skein

Crochet Hook

- ☐ Size I (5.5 mm)
  or size needed for gauge

Additional Supplies

- ☐ Yarn needle

SIZE INFORMATION

Small: 6-12 months

Medium: 12-18 months

Large: 18-24 months

Finished Scarf Measurement:

3½"h x 46½{47-47½}"w/
   9 cm x 118{119.5-120.5} cm

Size Note: We have printed
the instructions for the sizes in
different colors to make it easier
for you to find:
- Small in Blue
- Medium in Pink
- Large in Green

Instructions in Black apply to all
sizes.

GAUGE INFORMATION

In pattern, 2 repeats

(20 dc) = 5¼" (13.25 cm);

8 rows = 4½" (11.5 cm)

Gauge Swatch:

5½"w x 2¼"h (14 cm x 5.75 cm)

With Lavender, ch 23.

Row 1 (Right side): Dc in fourth ch from hook **(3 skipped chs count as first dc)** and in next ch, skip next 2 chs, 5 dc in next ch, skip next 2 chs, dc in next 5 chs, skip next 2 chs, 5 dc in next ch, skip next 2 chs, dc in last 3 chs: 21 dc.

Row 2: Ch 3 **(counts as first dc, now and throughout)**, turn; dc in next 2 dc, skip next 2 dc, 5 dc in next dc, skip next 2 dc, dc in next 5 dc, skip next 2 dc, 5 dc in next dc, skip next 2 dc, dc in last 3 dc.

Rows 3 and 4: Ch 3, turn; dc in next 7 dc, skip next 2 dc, 5 dc in next dc, skip next 2 dc, dc in last 8 dc.

Finish off.

INSTRUCTIONS
Hood

Size Small ONLY

With Lavender, ch 49; place a marker in third ch from hook for Scarf placement.

Row 1 (Right side): 5 Dc in sixth ch from hook **(5 skipped chs count as first dc plus 2 skipped chs)**, ★ skip next 2 chs, dc in next 5 chs, skip next 2 chs, 5 dc in next ch; repeat from ★ across to last 3 chs, skip next 2 chs, dc in last ch: 47 dc.

Sizes Medium & Large ONLY

With Lavender, ch {51-53}; place a marker in third ch from hook for Scarf placement.

Row 1 (Right side)**:** Dc in fourth ch from hook **(3 skipped chs count as first dc)**, dc in next {0-1} ch(s) *(see Zeros, page 39)*, skip next 2 chs, 5 dc in next ch, ★ skip next 2 chs, dc in next 5 chs, skip next 2 chs, 5 dc in next ch; repeat from ★ across to last {4-5} chs, skip next 2 chs, dc in last {2-3} chs: {49-51} dc.

All Sizes

Note: Loop a short piece of yarn around any stitch to mark Row 1 as **right** side.

Row 2: Ch 3 **(counts as first dc, now and throughout)**, turn; dc in next 0{1-2} dc *(see Zeros, page 39)*, skip next 2 dc, 5 dc in next dc, ★ skip next 2 dc, dc in next 5 dc, skip next 2 dc, 5 dc in next dc; repeat from ★ across to last 3{4-5} dc, skip next 2 dc, dc in last 1{2-3} dc.

Rows 3 and 4: Ch 3, turn; dc in next 5{6-7} dc, skip next 2 dc, 5 dc in next dc, ★ skip next 2 dc, dc in next 5 dc, skip next 2 dc, 5 dc in next dc; repeat from ★ across to last 8{9-10} dc, skip next 2 dc, dc in last 6{7-8} dc.

Rows 5 and 6: Ch 3, turn; dc in next 0{1-2} dc, skip next 2 dc, 5 dc in next dc, ★ skip next 2 dc, dc in next 5 dc, skip next 2 dc, 5 dc in next dc; repeat from ★ across to last 3{4-5} dc, skip next 2 dc, dc in last 1{2-3} dc.

Repeat Rows 3-6 for pattern until Hood measures approximately 6{7-8}"/15{18-20.5} cm from beginning ch.

Finish off, leaving a long end for sewing.

Thread yarn needle with long end and, with **wrong** side together, fold last row in half matching sts; sew sts together for top seam.

Scarf

Foundation Row: With Lavender, ch 65; with **wrong** side of Hood facing and 📹 working in free loops *(Fig. 2b, page 40)* and in sps of beginning ch, sc in marked ch and in next 0{1-2} ch(s), 2 sc in next sp, sc in next ch, 2 sc in next sp, ★ sc in next 5 chs, 2 sc in next sp, sc in next ch, 2 sc in next sp; repeat from ★ across to last 1{2-3} ch(s), sc in last 1{2-3} chs: 47{49-51} sc and 65 chs.

Size Small ONLY

Row 1 (Right side)**:** Ch 67, turn; 5 dc in sixth ch from hook **(5 skipped chs count as first dc plus 2 skipped chs)**, working in each ch and in each sc across, ★ skip next 2 sts, dc in next 5 sts, skip next 2 sts, 5 dc in next st; repeat from ★ across to last 3 chs, skip next 2 chs, dc in last ch: 177 dc.

Sizes Medium & Large ONLY

Row 1 (Right side)**:** Ch 67, turn; dc in fourth ch from hook **(3 skipped chs count as first dc)**, dc in next {0-1} ch(s), working in each ch and in each sc across, skip next 2 chs, 5 dc in next ch, ★ skip next 2 sts, dc in next 5 sts, skip next 2 sts, 5 dc in next st; repeat from ★ across to last {4-5} chs, skip next 2 chs, dc in last {2-3} chs: {179-181} dc.

All Sizes

Rows 2-6: Work same as Hood.

Finish off.

Edging

With **right** side of Scarf facing, 📹 join Variegated with sc in any corner *(see Joining With Sc, page 40)*; sc evenly around edge of Scarf and Hood working 3 sc in each corner; join with slip st to first sc, finish off.

LEG WARMERS

 **EASY +**

SHOPPING LIST

Yarn (Medium Weight)

[5 ounces, 256 yards
(141 grams, 234 meters) per skein]:

☐ Dk Red - 1 skein

☐ White - 1 skein

Crochet Hooks

☐ Size H (5 mm) **and**

☐ Size I (5.5 mm)

or sizes needed for gauge

SIZE INFORMATION

Finished Circumference:

Small (3-12 mos): 6¾" (17 cm)

Medium (12-18 mos)**:** 7³/₈"
(18.5 cm)

Large (18-24 mos): 7⁷/₈" (20 cm)

Finished Length:

Small (3-12 mos): 5" (12.5 cm)

Medium (12-18 mos)**:** 5¾"
(14.5 cm)

Large (18-24 mos): 5¾" (14.5 cm)

Size Note: We have printed
the instructions for the sizes in
different colors to make it easier
for you to find:

• Small in Blue

• Medium in Pink

• Large in Green

Instructions in Black apply to all
sizes.

GAUGE INFORMATION

With larger size hook, in pattern,
(Cluster, ch 1) 4 times = 2¼"
(5.75 cm); 6 rows = 2¾" (7 cm)

Gauge Swatch: 2½"w x 2¼"h
(6.25 cm x 5.75 cm)

With larger hook & Dk Red, ch 10.

Row 1: Sc in second ch from hook
and in each ch across: 9 sc.

Row 2 (Right side)**:** Ch 2, turn; [YO,
insert hook in first sc, YO and pull
up a loop, YO and draw through
2 loops on hook] twice, YO and
draw through all 3 loops on hook
(first Cluster made), ★ ch 1, skip
next sc, work Cluster in next sc;
repeat from ★ across: 5 Clusters
and 4 ch-1 sps.

Row 3: Ch 1, turn; sc in first Cluster
and in each ch-1 sp and Cluster
across: 9 sc.

Rows 4 and 5: Repeat Rows 2 and 3.
Finish off.

STITCH GUIDE

TREBLE CROCHET
(abbreviated tr)

YO twice, insert hook in st indicated, YO and pull up a loop (4 loops on hook), (YO and draw through 2 loops on hook) 3 times.

FRONT POST DOUBLE CROCHET (abbreviated FPdc)

YO, insert hook from **front** to **back** around post of st indicated (*Fig. 3, page 40*), YO and pull up a loop (3 loops on hook), (YO and draw through 2 loops on hook) twice.

BEGINNING CLUSTER
(uses one st)

Ch 2, ★ YO, insert hook in same st as joining, YO and pull up a loop, YO and draw through 2 loops on hook; repeat from ★ once **more**, YO and draw through all 3 loops on hook.

CLUSTER (uses one st)

★ YO, insert hook in st indicated, YO and pull up a loop, YO and draw through 2 loops on hook; repeat from ★ 2 times **more**, YO and draw through all 4 loops on hook.

INSTRUCTIONS

Leg Warmer (Make 2)

RIBBING

With smaller size hook and Dk Red, ch 24{26-28}; being careful **not** to twist ch, join with slip st to form a ring.

Rnd 1 (Right side)**:** Ch 3 (**counts as first dc, now and throughout**), dc in next ch and in each ch around; join with slip st to first dc: 24{26-28} dc.

Note: Loop a short piece of yarn around any stitch to mark Rnd 1 as **right** side.

Rnd 2: Ch 3, work FPdc around next dc, (dc in next dc, work FPdc around next dc) around; join with slip st to first dc: 12{13-14} dc and 12{13-14} FPdc.

Rnd 3: Ch 3, work FPdc around next FPdc, (dc in next dc, work FPdc around next FPdc) around, drop Dk Red; 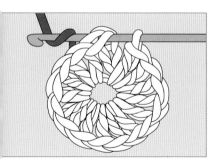 with White, join with slip st to first dc *(Fig. A)*, do **not** finish off.

Fig. A

BODY

Change to larger size hook.

Rnd 1: Work Beginning Cluster, ch 1, skip next FPdc, ★ work Cluster in next dc, ch 1, skip next FPdc; repeat from ★ around, drop White; with Dk Red, join with slip st to top of Beginning Cluster: 12{13-14} Clusters and 12{13-14} ch-1 sps.

Rnd 2: Ch 1, sc in same st as joining and in next ch-1 sp, (sc in next Cluster and in next ch-1 sp) around, drop Dk Red; with White, join with slip st to first sc: 24{26-28} sc.

Rnd 3: Work Beginning Cluster, ch 1, skip next sc, ★ work Cluster in next sc, ch 1, skip next sc; repeat from ★ around, drop White; with Dk Red, join with slip st to top of Beginning Cluster: 12{13-14} Clusters and 12{13-14} ch-1 sps.

Rnd 4: Ch 1, sc in same st as joining and in next ch-1 sp, (sc in next Cluster and in next ch-1 sp) around, drop Dk Red; with White, join with slip st to first sc: 24{26-28} sc.

Repeat Rnds 3 and 4, 0{1-1} time(s) *(see Zeros, page 39)*.

Next Rnd: With smaller size hook, work Beginning Cluster, ch 1, skip next sc, ★ work Cluster in next sc, ch 1, skip next sc; repeat from ★ around, cut White; with Dk Red, join with slip st to top of Beginning Cluster: 12{13-14} Clusters and 12{13-14} ch-1 sps.

Last Rnd: Ch 1, sc in same st as joining and in next ch-1 sp, (sc in next Cluster and in next ch-1 sp) around; join with slip st to Back Loop Only of first sc *(Fig. 1, page 40)*, do **not** finish off: 24{26-28} sc.

RUFFLE

Rnd 1: Ch 4 (**counts as first tr**), tr in Back Loop Only of same st as joining, 2 tr in Back Loop Only of next sc and each sc around; join with slip st to first tr, finish off.

Rnd 2: With **right** side facing, Ribbing toward you, and using smaller size hook, join White with sc *(see Joining With Sc, page 40)* in free loop of any sc on Last Rnd of Body *(Fig. 2a, page 40)*; working in free loops, sc in same st as joining, 2 dc in next sc, (2 sc in next sc, 2 dc in next sc) around; join with slip st to first sc, finish off.

FINGERLESS MITTS

 **EASY**

Yarn (Medium Weight)
[3.5 ounces, 175 yards
(141 grams, 160 meters) per
skein]:

☐ 1 skein

Crochet Hooks

☐ Size H (5 mm) **and**

☐ Size I (5.5 mm)

or sizes needed for gauge

SIZE INFORMATION

Finished Circumference:

Small (3-12 mos): 4½" (11.5 cm)

Medium (12-18 mos): 5⅛" (13 cm)

Large (18-24 mos): 5¾" (14.5 cm)

Finished Length:

Small (3-12 mos): 3½" (9 cm)

Medium (12-18 mos): 3½" (9 cm)

Large (18-24 mos): 3¾" (9.5 cm)

Size Note: We have printed the
instructions for the sizes in different
colors to make it easier for you to find:

• Small in Blue

• Medium in Pink

• Large in Green

Instructions in Black apply to all sizes.

GAUGE INFORMATION

With larger size hook, 14 sc and
   14 rows/rnds = 4" (10 cm)

Gauge Swatch: 2" (5 cm) square
With larger size hook, ch 8.

Row 1: Sc in second ch from hook
and in each ch across: 7 sc.

Rows 2-7: Ch 1, turn; sc in each sc
across.
Finish off.

INSTRUCTIONS

Mitt (Make 2)

BODY

With smaller size hook and
beginning at wrist, ch 16{18-20};
being careful **not** to twist ch, join
with slip st to form a ring.

Rnd 1 (Right side)**:** Ch 1, sc in
same ch as joining and in each ch
around; join with slip st to first sc:
16{18-20} sc.

Rnd 2: Ch 1, sc in same st as joining
and in each sc around; join with
slip st to first sc.

Rnd 3: Ch 3 (**counts as first dc**), dc in next sc and in each sc around; join with slip st to first dc.

Rnd 4: Ch 1, sc in same st as joining and in each dc around; join with slip st to first sc.

Change to larger size hook.

Rnds 5 thru 6{6-7}: Ch 1, sc in same st as joining and in each sc around; join with slip st to first sc, do **not** finish off.

Thumb Opening
Rnd 1: Ch 1, sc in same st as joining and in next 5 sc, ch 3, skip next 3 sc (thumb opening), sc in last 7{9-11} sc; join with slip st to first sc: 13{15-17} sc and one ch-3 sp.

Rnd 2: Ch 1, sc in same st as joining and in next 5 sc, 3 sc in next ch-3 sp, sc in last 7{9-11} sc; join with slip st to first sc: 16{18-20} sc.

Rnd 3: Ch 1, sc in same st as joining and in each sc around; join with slip st to first sc.

Sizes Small & Large ONLY
Edging: Ch 1, sc in same st as joining and in next sc, ch 1, dc in next 2 sc, ch 1, ★ sc in next 2 sc, ch 1, dc in next 2 sc, ch 1; repeat from ★ around; join with slip st to first sc, finish off.

Size Medium ONLY
Edging: Ch 1, 2 sc in same st as joining, † ch 1, dc in next 2 sc, ch 1, sc in next 2 sc, ch 1, dc in next 2 sc, ch 1 †, sc in next 2 sc, ch 1, dc in next 2 sc, ch 1, 2 sc in next sc, repeat from † to † once; join with slip st to first sc, finish off.

TIE
With smaller size hook, chain a 14{14½-15}"/ 35.5{37-38} cm length; finish off.

Using photo as a guide, weave Tie through dc on Rnd 3; tie into a bow.

SLOUCHY BEANIE

 **EASY**

SHOPPING LIST

Yarn (Light Weight)
[5 ounces, 362 yards
(140 grams, 331 meters) per
skein]:

☐ 1 skein

Crochet Hooks

☐ Size F (3.75 mm) **and**

☐ Size H (5 mm)

or sizes needed for gauge

SIZE INFORMATION

Fits Head Circumference:

Small (3-12 mos)**:** 11" (28 cm)

Medium (12-18 mos)**:** 13½"
(34.5 cm)

Large (18-24 mos)**:** 16" (40.5 cm)

Size Note: We have printed
the instructions for the sizes in
different colors to make it easier
for you to find:

Small in Blue

Medium in Pink

Large in Green

Instructions in Black apply to all
sizes.

GAUGE INFORMATION

With larger size hook, in pattern,

14 dc and = 3" (7.5 cm);

6 rnds = 2½" (6.25 cm)

Gauge Swatch: 2¾" (7 cm)

With larger size hook, ch 5; join
with slip st to form a ring.

Rnd 1 (Right side)**:** Ch 3 (**counts
as first dc, now and throughout**),
11 dc in ring; join with slip st to
first dc: 12 dc.

Rnd 2: Ch 3, dc in next dc, ch 3,
🎥 work 3 dc around post of last
dc made, ★ dc in next 2 dc, ch 3,
work 3 dc around post of last dc
made; repeat from ★ around; join
with slip st to first dc, finish off:
30 dc and 6 ch-3 sps.

STITCH GUIDE

FRONT POST DOUBLE CROCHET *(abbreviated FPdc)*
YO, insert hook from **front** to **back** around post of st indicated *(Fig. 3, page 40)*, YO and pull up a loop (3 loops on hook), (YO and draw through 2 loops on hook) twice.

INSTRUCTIONS
Body

With larger size hook, ch 5; join with slip st to form a ring.

Rnd 1 (Right side)**:** Ch 3 (**counts as first dc, now and throughout**), 7{9-11} dc in ring; join with slip st to first dc: 8{10-12} dc.

Rnd 2: Ch 3, dc in next dc, ch 3, work 3 dc around post of last dc made, ★ dc in next 2 dc, ch 3, work 3 dc around post of last dc made; repeat from ★ around; join with slip st to first dc: 20{25-30} dc and 4{5-6} ch-3 sps.

Rnd 3: Ch 3, 2 dc in same st as joining, ch 2, sc in next ch-3 sp, ch 2, skip next 3 dc, ★ 3 dc in next dc, ch 2, sc in next ch-3 sp, ch 2, skip next 3 dc; repeat from ★ around; join with slip st to first dc: 16{20-24} sts and 8{10-12} ch-2 sps.

Rnd 4: Ch 3, dc in next 2 dc, 3 dc in next ch-2 sp, dc in next sc, 3 dc in next ch-2 sp, ★ dc in next 3 dc, 3 dc in next ch-2 sp, dc in next sc, 3 dc in next ch-2 sp; repeat from ★ around; join with slip st to first dc: 40{50-60} dc.

Rnd 5: Ch 3, skip next dc, dc in next dc, ch 3, work 4 dc around post of last dc made, skip next 2 dc, ★ dc in next dc, skip next dc, dc in next dc, ch 3, work 4 dc around post of last dc made, skip next 2 dc; repeat from ★ around; join with slip st to first dc: 48{60-72} dc and 8{10-12} ch-3 sps.

Rnd 6: Ch 3, dc in same st as joining, ch 2, sc in next ch-3 sp, ch 2, skip next 4 dc, ★ 2 dc in next dc, ch 2, sc in next ch-3 sp, ch 2, skip next 4 dc; repeat from ★ around; join with slip st to first dc: 24{30-36} sts and 16{20-24} ch-2 sps.

Rnd 7: Ch 3, dc in next dc and in next ch-2 sp, 2 dc in next sc, dc in next ch-2 sp, ★ dc in next 2 dc and in next ch-2 sp, 2 dc in next sc, dc in next ch-2 sp; repeat from ★ around; join with slip st to first dc: 48{60-72} dc.

Rnd 8: Ch 3, skip next 2 dc, dc in next dc, ch 3, work 4 dc around post of last dc made, skip next 2 dc, ★ dc in next dc, skip next 2 dc, dc in next dc, ch 3, work 4 dc around post of last dc made, skip next 2 dc; repeat from ★ around; join with slip st to first dc: 48{60-72} dc and 8{10-12} ch-3 sps.

Rnd 9: Ch 3, dc in same st as joining, ch 2, 2 sc in next ch-3 sp, ch 2, skip next 4 dc, ★ 2 dc in next dc, ch 2, 2 sc in next ch-3 sp, ch 2, skip next 4 dc; repeat from ★ around; join with slip st to first dc: 32{40-48} sts and 16{20-24} ch-2 sps.

Rnd 10: Ch 3, dc in next dc and in next ch-2 sp, dc in next 2 sc and in next ch-2 sp, ★ dc in next 2 dc and in next ch-2 sp, dc in next 2 sc and in next ch-2 sp; repeat from ★ around; join with slip st to first dc: 48{60-72} dc.

Rnd 11: Ch 3, skip next 2 dc, dc in next dc, ch 3, work 4 dc around post of last dc made, skip next 2 dc, ★ dc in next dc, skip next 2 dc, dc in next dc, ch 3, work 4 dc around post of last dc made, skip next 2 dc; repeat from ★ around; join with slip st to first dc: 48{60-72} dc and 8{10-12} ch-3 sps.

Size Large ONLY
Rnds 12-14: Repeat Rnds 9-11: 72 dc and 12 ch-3 sps.

All Sizes
Last Rnd: With smaller size hook, ch 3, dc in same st as joining, ch 2, 2 sc in next ch-3 sp, ch 2, skip next 4 dc, ★ 2 dc in next dc, ch 2, 2 sc in next ch-3 sp, ch 2, skip next 4 dc; repeat from ★ around; join with slip st to first dc, do **not** finish off: 32{40-48} sts and 16{20-24} ch-2 sps.

Band

Rnd 1: Ch 3, dc in next dc and in next ch-2 sp, dc in next 2 sc and in next ch-2 sp, ★ dc in next 2 dc and in next ch-2 sp, dc in next 2 sc and in next ch-2 sp; repeat from ★ around; join with slip st to first dc: 48{60-72} dc.

Rnd 2: Ch 3, dc in next dc, work FPdc around next dc, (dc in next 2 dc, work FPdc around next dc) around; join with slip st to first dc.

Rnds 3 and 4: Ch 3, dc in next dc, work FPdc around next FPdc, (dc in next 2 dc, work FPdc around next FPdc) around; join with slip st to first dc.

Finish off.

HAT WITH FLOWER

EASY

SIZE INFORMATION

Finished Band Circumference:

Small (3-12 mos): 12" (30.5 cm)

Medium (12-18 mos): 14½" (37 cm)

Large (18-24 mos): 16¾" (42.5 cm)

Size Note: We have printed the
instructions for the sizes in different
colors to make it easier for you to find:

• Small in Blue

• Medium in Pink

• Large in Green

Instructions in Black apply to all
sizes.

GAUGE INFORMATION

10 sc and 12 rows = 3" (7.5 cm)

Gauge Swatch:

2¾" (7 cm) diameter

With White, ch 4; join with slip st to
form a ring.

Rnd 1 (Right side)**:** Ch 3 **(counts
as first dc, now and throughout),**
11 dc in ring; join with slip st to
first dc: 12 dc.

Rnd 2: Ch 3, dc in same st as
joining, 2 dc in next dc and in each
dc around; join with slip st to first
dc, finish off: 24 dc.

INSTRUCTIONS
Body

With White, ch 4; join with slip st to
form a ring.

Rnd 1 (Right side)**:** Ch 3 **(counts
as first dc, now and throughout),**
9{11-13} dc in ring; join with slip st
to first dc: 10{12-14} dc.

Note: Loop a short piece of yarn around any stitch to mark Rnd 1 as **right** side.

Rnd 2: Ch 3, dc in same st as joining, 2 dc in next dc and in each dc around; join with slip st to first dc: 20{24-28} dc.

Rnd 3: Ch 1, sc in same st as joining, ch 3, skip next dc, ★ sc in next dc, ch 3, skip next dc; repeat from ★ around; join with slip st to first sc: 10{12-14} ch-3 sps.

Rnd 4: (Slip st, ch 3, 2 dc) in next ch-3 sp, 3 dc in next ch-3 sp and in each ch-3 sp around; join with slip st to first dc: 30{36-42} dc.

Rnd 5: (Slip st, ch 1, sc) in next dc, ch 4, skip next 2 dc, ★ sc in next dc, ch 4, skip next 2 sts; repeat from ★ around; join with slip st to first sc: 10{12-14} ch-4 sps.

Rnd 6: (Slip st, ch 3, 3 dc) in next ch-4 sp, (ch 1, 4 dc in next ch-4 sp) around, sc in first dc to form last ch-1 sp: 40{48-56} dc and 10{12-14} ch-1 sps.

Rnd 7: Ch 1, sc in last ch-1 sp made, ch 4, (2 sc in next ch-1 sp, ch 4) around, sc in same sp as first sc; join with slip st to first sc: 10{12-14} ch-4 sps.

Rnds 8 thru 9{11-13}: Repeat Rnds 6 and 7, 1{2-3} time(s): 10{12-14} ch-4 sps.

Rnd 10{12-14}: (Slip st, ch 3, 3 dc) in next ch-4 sp, ch 1, (4 dc in next ch-4 sp, ch 1) around; join with slip st to first dc, do **not** finish off: 40{48-56} dc and 10{12-14} ch-1 sps.

Band

Rnd 1: Ch 1, sc in same st as joining and in next 3 dc, skip next ch-1 sp, (sc in next 4 dc, skip next ch-1 sp) around; join with slip st to first sc: 40{48-56} sc.

Rnds 2-4: Ch.1, sc in same st as joining and in each sc around; join with slip st to first sc.

Finish off.

Flower

With Yellow and leaving a long end for sewing, ch 35.

Row 1: Dc in fifth ch from hook **(4 skipped chs count as first dc plus ch 1)**, ch 1, ★ skip next ch, (dc, ch 1) twice in next ch; repeat from ★ across to last 2 chs, skip next ch, (dc, ch 1, dc) in last ch: 32 dc and 31 ch-1 sps.

Row 2 (Right side)**:** Ch 1, turn; (sc, hdc, 2 dc, hdc, sc) in first ch-1 sp, ★ skip next ch-1 sp, (sc, hdc, 2 dc, hdc, sc) in next ch-1 sp; repeat from ★ across; finish off.

Note: Mark Row 2 as **right** side.

Thread yarn needle with beginning end and weave through beginning ch. Pull end tightly to form Flower and tack petals in place; secure end.

Using photo as a guide for placement, sew **wrong** side of Flower to **right** side of Hat.

BLANKET

 **EASY**

SHOPPING LIST

Yarn (Bulky Weight)

[1.76 ounces, 63 yards
(50 grams, 57 meters) per skein]:
☐ 3 skeins

Crochet Hook
☐ Size L (8 mm)
  or size needed for gauge

Finished Size:
   20½" (52 cm) square

GAUGE INFORMATION

In pattern, (2 dc, ch 2) 3
   times = 4¾" (12 cm);
   4 rnds = 3¾" (9.5 cm)
Gauge Swatch: 4" (10 cm) square
Work instructions through Rnd 2:
24 dc and 12 sps.

INSTRUCTIONS

Ch 5; join with slip st to form a ring

Rnd 1 (Right side)**:** Ch 6 **(counts
as first dc plus ch 3, now and
throughout)**, 2 dc in ring, ch 2,
★ (2 dc, ch 3, 2 dc) in ring, ch 2;
repeat from ★ 2 times **more**, dc
in ring; join with slip st to first dc:
16 dc and 8 sps.

Rnd 2: (Slip st, ch 6, 2 dc) in next
ch-3 sp, ch 2, 2 dc in next ch-2 sp,
ch 2, ★ (2 dc, ch 3, 2 dc) in next
ch-3 sp, ch 2, 2 dc in next ch-2 sp,
ch 2; repeat from ★ 2 times **more**,
dc in same sp as first slip st; join
with slip st to first dc: 24 dc and
12 sps.

Rnd 3: (Slip st, ch 6, 2 dc) in next
ch-3 sp, ch 2, (2 dc in next ch-2 sp,
ch 2) twice, ★ (2 dc, ch 3, 2 dc) in
next ch-3 sp, ch 2, (2 dc in next
ch-2 sp, ch 2) twice; repeat from ★
2 times **more**, dc in same sp as first
slip st; join with slip st to first dc:
32 dc and 16 sps.

Rnds 4-11: (Slip st, ch 6, 2 dc) in next ch-3 sp, ch 2, ★ (2 dc in next ch-2 sp, ch 2) across to next ch-3 sp, (2 dc, ch 3, 2 dc) in next ch-3 sp, ch 2; repeat from ★ 2 times **more**, (2 dc in next ch-2 sp, ch 2) across, dc in same sp as first slip st; join with slip st to first dc: 96 dc and 48 sps.

Rnd 12: (Slip st, ch 6, 2 dc) in next ch-3 sp, (sc, 2 dc, sc) in each of next 11 ch-2 sps, ★ (2 dc, ch 3, 2 dc) in next ch-3 sp, (sc, 2 dc, sc) in each of next 11 ch-2 sps; repeat from ★ 2 times **more**, dc in same sp as first slip st; join with slip st to first dc, finish off.

GENERAL INSTRUCTIONS

ABBREVIATIONS

ch(s)	chain(s)
cm	centimeters
dc	double crochet(s)
dc2tog	double crochet 2 together
FPdc	Front Post double crochet(s)
hdc	half double crochet(s)
mm	millimeters
mos	months
Rnd(s)	Round(s)
sc	single crochet(s)
sc2tog	single crochet 2 together
sp(s)	space(s)
st(s)	stitch(es)
tr	treble crochet(s)
YO	yarn over

SYMBOLS & TERMS

★ — work instructions following ★ as many **more** times as indicated in addition to the first time.

† to † — work all instructions from first † to second † **as many** times as specified.

( ) or **[ ]** — work enclosed instructions **as many** times as specified by the number immediately following **or** work all enclosed instructions in the stitch or space indicated **or** contains explanatory remarks.

colon (:) — the number(s) given after a colon at the end of a row or round denote(s) the number of stitches or spaces you should have on that row or round.

CROCHET TERMINOLOGY		
UNITED STATES		INTERNATIONAL
slip stitch (slip st)	=	single crochet (sc)
single crochet (sc)	=	double crochet (dc)
half double crochet (hdc)	=	half treble crochet (htr)
double crochet (dc)	=	treble crochet(tr)
treble crochet (tr)	=	double treble crochet (dtr)
double treble crochet (dtr)	=	triple treble crochet (ttr)
triple treble crochet (tr tr)	=	quadruple treble crochet (qtr)
skip	=	miss

■□□□ BEGINNER		Projects for first-time crocheters using basic stitches. Minimal shaping.
■■□□ EASY		Projects using yarn with basic stitches, repetitive stitch patterns, simple color changes, and simple shaping and finishing.
■■■□ INTERMEDIATE		Projects using a variety of techniques, such as basic lace patterns or color patterns, mid-level shaping and finishing.
■■■■ EXPERIENCED		Projects with intricate stitch patterns, techniques and dimension, such as non-repeating patterns, multi-color techniques, fine threads, small hooks, detailed shaping and refined finishing.

GAUGE

Exact gauge is **essential** for proper size. Before beginning your project, make the sample swatch given in the individual instructions in the yarn and hook specified. After completing the swatch, measure it, counting your stitches and rows or rounds carefully. If your swatch is larger or smaller than specified, **make another, changing hook size to get the correct gauge**. Keep trying until you find the size hook that will give you the specified gauge.

ZEROS

Zeros are sometimes used so that all sizes can be combined. For example, repeat Rnds 3 and 4, 0{1-1} time(s) means the first size would do nothing and the middle and last sizes would repeat Rnds 3 and 4 once.

Yarn Weight Symbol & Names	LACE 0	SUPER FINE 1	FINE 2	LIGHT 3	MEDIUM 4	BULKY 5	SUPER BULKY 6
Type of Yarns in Category	Fingering, 10-count crochet thread	Sock, Fingering Baby	Sport, Baby	DK, Light Worsted	Worsted, Afghan, Aran	Chunky, Craft, Rug	Bulky, Roving
Crochet Gauge* Ranges in Single Crochet to 4" (10 cm)	32-42 double crochets**	21-32 sts	16-20 sts	12-17 sts	11-14 sts	8-11 sts	5-9 sts
Advised Hook Size Range	Steel*** 6,7,8 Regular hook B-1	B-1 to E-4	E-4 to 7	7 to I-9	I-9 to K-10.5	K-10.5 to M-13	M-13 and larger

*GUIDELINES ONLY: The chart above reflects the most commonly used gauges and hook sizes for specific yarn categories.

** Lace weight yarns are usually crocheted on larger-size hooks to create lacy openwork patterns. Accordingly, a gauge range is difficult to determine. Always follow the gauge stated in your pattern.

*** Steel crochet hooks are sized differently from regular hooks—the higher the number the smaller the hook, which is the reverse of regular hook sizing.

CROCHET HOOKS																
U.S.	B-1	C-2	D-3	E-4	F-5	G-6	H-8	I-9	J-10	K-10½	L-11	M/N-13	N/P-15	P/Q	Q	S
Metric - mm	2.25	2.75	3.25	3.5	3.75	4	5	5.5	6	6.5	8	9	10	15	16	19

JOINING WITH SC

When instructed to join with sc, begin with a slip knot on the hook. Insert the hook in the stitch or space indicated, YO and pull up a loop, YO and draw through both loops on the hook.

JOINING WITH DC

When instructed to join with dc, begin with a slip knot on the hook. YO, holding loop on the hook, insert the hook in the stitch or space indicated, YO and pull up a loop (3 loops on hook), (YO and draw through 2 loops on hook) twice.

BACK LOOP ONLY

Work only in loop(s) indicated by arrow (Fig. 1).

Fig. 1

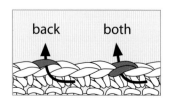

FREE LOOPS

After working in Back Loops Only on a row or round, there will be a ridge of unused loops. Later, when instructed to work in free loops of the same row or round, work in these loops (Fig. 2a).

When instructed to work in free loops of a chain, work in loop indicated by arrow (Fig. 2b).

Fig. 2a   **Fig. 2b**

POST STITCH

Work around post of stitch indicated, inserting hook in direction of arrow (Fig. 3).

Fig. 3

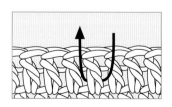